Berkeley, more than Paris, more than either Cambridge — more certainly than Palo Alto — has now and for decades been known as the place where things begin.

John Kenneth Galbraith

6   *Sather Tower (The Campanile)*

THE UNIVERSITY OF

CALIFORNIA

BERKELEY

PHOTOGRAPHED BY JAMES A. SUGAR

HARMONY HOUSE

PUBLISHERS LOUISVILLE

We would like to thank the many kind and talented people of the
California Alumni Association for all their help in the logistics,
production and review phases of this book. Special thanks to
Executive Director Mike Koll ; Associate Executive Director
Kees Van Der Zee ; Bonnie King, Coordinator of Membership
Services ; Bill Reichle, Alumni Field Director ; Russell
Schoch, Editor, California Monthly ; William M. Roberts,
University Archivist, The Bancroft Library ; and Marie
Thornton, Assistant University Archivist.

Executive Editors: William Butler and William Strode
Library of Congress Catalog Number 86-082732
Hardcover International Standard Book Number 0-916509-10-9
Printed in USA by Pinaire Lithographing Corp., Louisville, Kentucky
First Edition printed March, 1987 by Harmony House Publishers
P.O.Box 90, Prospect, Kentucky 40059 (502) 228-2010 / 228-4446

INTRODUCTION

By Russell Schoch, Editor
California Monthly

That the University of California is a special place is easily seen today, when the Berkeley campus is recognized as one of the world's greatest centers of learning, when its graduate programs are consistently certified as the best in the nation, and when its string of Nobel Laureates is longer and brighter than those of most nations, let alone other college campuses.

But this sense of specialness was present at the beginning, more than a century ago. It was just after California had achieved statehood, and the county of Alameda had been incorporated, when a group of educators was charged with selecting the best site for a permanent place of learning on the Pacific coast.

Let us listen to a 19th-century account of that successful search, conducted by the Reverend Henry Durant, who was to become the first president of the University of California. He had journeyed far and wide in search of the perfect setting: "One morning in spring, when the air, purified by the rains of winter, brought in clear relief the lines of ocean, valley, hill and mountain, when the trees were budding and the turf was green, and a vague, dark spot in the sunlight — the Farallon Islands — showed itself through the Golden Gate, he passed through fields unbroken by roads, untrodden by man, and came to the present site of Berkeley. 'Eureka!' he exclaimed, 'Eureka! I have found it. I have found it.' "

What Durant had found, then so pristine and "untrodden by man," is what generations of Cal students since the 1870s have known and cherished as the campus of the University of California.

On march 23, 1868 -- Charter Day -- the legislature and the governor of the State of California created the University of California, which was to be a "complete university," instructing the youth of the state in humanities as well as agriculture, mining, and mechanics.

What to name the townsite? After prolonged deliberation by the leaders of the movement for this "complete university," the land surrounding the new campus was named for George Berkeley, Bishop of Cloyne, who had visited America in 1789 in the hope of founding an educational institution for the betterment of "aboriginal Americans." His specific plans were never realized, but his name lives on, connected to a University that in some measure has captured the sweep and drama of Berkeley's poem, "On the Prospect of Planting Arts and Learning in America," the final stanza of which holds a special meaning for Californians:

Westward the course of empire takes its way;
The first four acts already past.
A fifth shall close the drama with the day;
Time's noblest offspring is the last.

And so all of the elements were in place for the opening of the University of California, on a site scarcely matched in beauty, connected to a name then hopeful of and now synonymous with excellence in education, and brought to fruition by a group of visionaries who saw to it that a strong university would grow and prosper with the new State of California.

Once the first two buildings (North Hall and South Hall) had been completed, the first students of the University

of California began their studies in Berkeley, in 1873. In speaking of these times of origin, it is important to note what the new University decided *not* to do. Differing from the practice of most American universities in this period, it would not be church-affiliated. And, after initially excluding women (the University's first class, the "Twelve Apostles," was all male) and imposing tuition, the Board of Regents opened the door to women and closed the door to tuition — a decision that remains in effect to this day. (Although "incidental fees" were early and continue to be charged.)

Much emphasis is placed — some would say misplaced — on athletics and athletic rivalries, especially with arch-rival Stanford. But most historians agree that the opening in 1891 of Leland Stanford Jr. University, on the Stanford farm in Palo Alto, was crucial to the development of a sense of cohesion for the young University of California. In 1892 the first football contest between the two schools was played — the first Big Game; 90 years later, in 1982, five laterals among four players with four seconds left (The Play) gave California a victory in one of the greatest of Big Games. What this history suggests is that a keen rivalry, in the classroom and on the field, between two such schools can be an important spur to excellence.

Private gifts began in the early days of the University and helped it mightily to prosper. In 1891, Mrs. Phoebe Apperson Hearst provided five scholarships for "worthy young women" attending the University. Mrs. Hearst's support of the campus was continued by her provision of funds both for the University's first comprehensive building plan and for key buildings, including the Hearst Memorial Mining Building and the Greek Theatre. Mrs. Jane K. Sather endowed two professorships and gave to the campus two of its enduring landmarks, Sather Tower (the Campanile) and Sather Gate.

As the 20th century opened, the distinguished scholar and vigorous administrator Benjamin Ide Wheeler was in charge of the young University of California. When President Wheeler was introduced to the students, he concluded his remarks with these stirring and well-remembered words about the University: "And so I say, cheer for her; it will do your lungs good. Love her; it will do your heart and life good." When he arrived, the University enrolled 2,600 students; when he left, in 1919, that number had tripled.

By the 1920s, the University of California had become the world's largest university, with 14,061 full-time students. But it was still considered, and properly so, a lively but predominantly regional institution. It had not yet achieved even nation-wide eminence. That began to change in the next decades, and two leaders—one an administrator, the other a scientist — were keys to the rise of the University of California during this period. The administrator was the first native Californian and the first alumnus of the University to be named its president: Robert Gordon Sproul '13. The scientist was the inventor of the cyclotron, a young man who earned his Ph.D. from Yale and then astounded the academic world by choosing Berkeley for his academic career: Ernest O. Lawrence.

Lawrence became the first person from a state university to win the Nobel Prize (in Physics, in 1939) and helped to gather a group of outstanding chemists and physicists at what was to be named the Lawrence Berkeley Laboratory, now one of the world's leading centers for research and education. Sproul, one of the most personable and magnetic figures in higher education in this century, oversaw not only Lawrence's work but the growth and maturity of the University as a whole.

Following World War II and the University of California's key role in its succesful conclusion, the world changed in many ways. One simple, yet dramatic, way was in the mode of transportation now available to academics throughout the world. The airplane, and the national and international conferences that followed in its wake, meant that no campus was isolated, that knowledge truly was a world-wide event. Also, the early 1950s saw a great expansion in the State of California — not only in its population but in the financial support it provided for its prized University system.

It was Clark Kerr, who also had earned a degree at Berkeley (Ph.D., 1939) who was president of the University in its heyday of expansion, the late 1950s and early 1960s, when the University system expanded to its current number of nine campuses.

Following the growth of this "multi-university" came protests throughout the country and centered on the Civil Rights Movement and the war in Viet Nam. The University of California, and Berkeley in particular, were important sites and targets of the activities of the late 1960s and early 1970s. Those were not easy times. Many traditional ties were broken — between students and faculty, faculty and faculty, and the University and the public — and it took a good decade for the effects of this period to diminish.

In 1980 Ira Michael Heyman became chancellor of the Berkeley campus, and in 1983 David P. Gardner, M.A. '59, Ph.D. '66, became president of the nine-campus system. The 1980s saw an expansion of good will and of financial support for the University, new top ratings for the school's educational programs, and an enormous increase in applications and enrollments for the University.

Thus, as the University of California settles into its second century and as the 21st century approaches, the University of California, which grew up and prospered with the state that called it into being, has every reason to claim its time-honored special place in the heart of all Californians.

Bechtel Engineering Center

1849 California's first Constitutional Convention calls for establishment of state university.

1860 Future campus site named "Berkeley" for George Berkeley, Bishop of Cloyne.

1868 Gov. Haight signs act creating the University of California.

1869 UC opens its doors in Oakland.

1870 Henry Durant becomes first president.

1872 Daniel Coit Gilman becomes second president; College of Chemistry established; first Alumni Association formed.

1873 University graduates first class; instruction begins at Berkeley as North and South Halls are completed.

1878 A.K.P. Harmon provides funds for Harmon Gymnasium.

1881 Bacon Library Building constructed; Mills Chair in philosophy donated.

1892 The first Big Game between Stanford and Cal is played — Cal loses 14 - 0.

1895 Charles Mills Gayley composes the song "The Golden Bear".

1896 Phoebe Apperson Hearst finances mining building as a memorial to her late husband.

1898 Cora Jane Flood provides funds to establish the College of Commerce, later the School of Business Administration.

1899 The Stanford Axe first appears at baseball game between Cal and Stanford.

1899 Benjamin Ide Wheeler becomes the eighth president of the University of California.

1900 Jane K. Sather establishes a trust to build Sather Gate and Sather Tower.

1903 John Galen Howard begins executing the campus architectural plan; The Hearst Greek

BERKELEY'S PAST

Theatre used for first time when President Roosevelt delivers Commencement Address.

1905 The "Big C" is constructed on Charter Hill.

1911 A bequest from Charles Franklin Doe is used to build Doe Library; Ernest V. Cowell leaves the University $250,000 to build hospital.

1920 Andy Smith's Wonder Team wins the first of four Pacific Coast Conference titles.

1923 California Memorial Stadium built.

1924 Haviland Hall is built to house School of Education, from gift of Hannah N. Haviland.

1927 Hearst gift builds Hearst Gymnasium .

1928 Ernest O. Lawrence comes to Berkeley to work on the cyclotron.

1928 Cal crew wins three Olympic gold

1930 Robert Gordon Sproul becomes the 11th president of the University of California.

1939 Ernest O. Lawrence awarded the Nobel Prize in Physics (the first at Berkeley).

1947 "Pappy" Waldorf comes to coach football.

1952 Clark Kerr becomes the first Chancellor of the Berkeley campus.

1954 The Alumni House is built.

1959 New Student Union building completed.

1966 UC Berkeley ranked #1 in nation for quality of graduate programs (also awarded to UC in 1970 and 1982). Bancroft Library refurbished.

1969 Zellerbach Hall completed with funds from the family of Isadore Zellerbach.

1970 The University A M

Teaching is the one activity professed by man which has the future for its single object. And what is true of any university wherever established is twice true on this farthest coast of the American continent. The west was always the direction of the future in America, and the University of California was built to face the future, if a university ever was.

Archibald MacLeish, Charter Day address, 1943

The Cyclotron

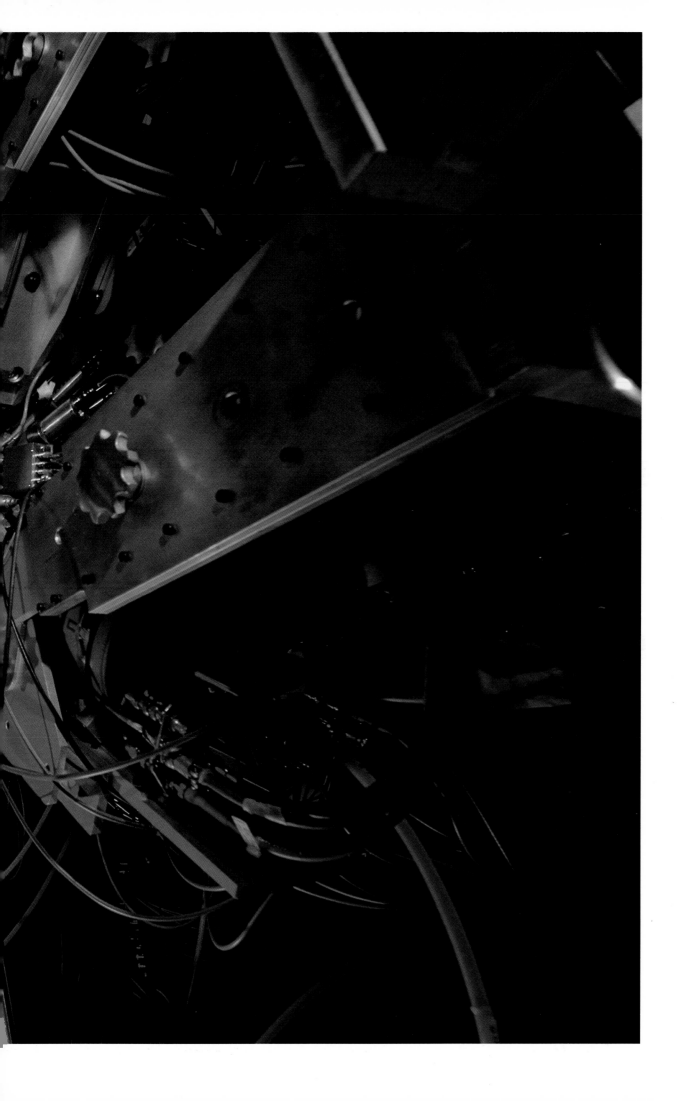

Hearst Memorial Mining Building

When I observe the men who surround me in Washington — when I reflect that the Secretary of State, the Secretary of Defense, the Chairman of the Atomic Energy Commission, the Director of the CIA and the Ambassador to India are all graduates or former students of this university .... I am forced to confront an uncomfortable truth, and so are you: that the New Frontier may well owe more to Berkeley than to Harvard.

President John F. Kennedy, 1962

In the past, I have spoken of California as the crucible for the nation. I would take that metaphor one step further, and speak of the University of California as the catalyst in the crucible.

Rudolph A. Peterson, President, Bank of America, 1968

Life Sciences Building

University Art Museum

We are a family. You cannot make a university out of minds and brains. In a university, as elsewhere in the world, heart is more than head, love is more than reason. Hold fast to that love for the University.

Benjamin Ide Wheeler

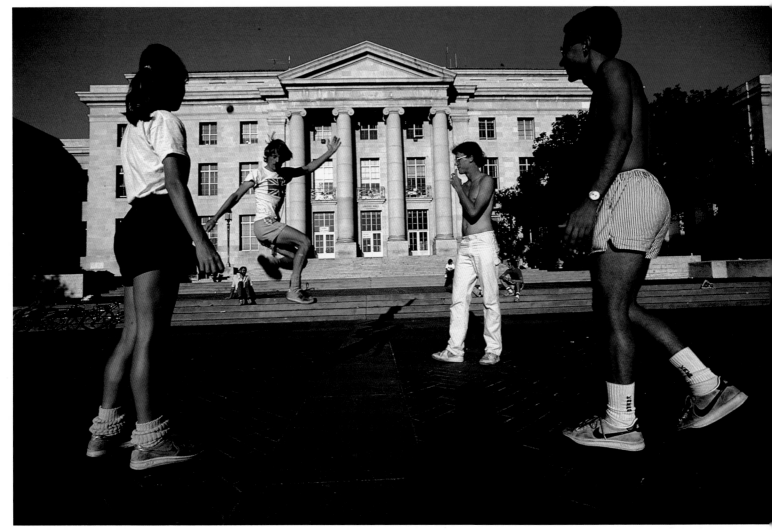

Sproul Plaza

The University of California was conceived in the great academic tradition and born to high intellectual adventure. The spirit of free inquiry has never faltered within its walls, nor has faith in intelligence weakened .... Even in far and foreign lands it has justified its motto — "Let there be light."

Robert G. Sproul, 1956

Strawberry Creek

Hearst Gymnasium

Recreational Sports Facility

Yours is one of the great universities of the world. Your system of higher education here in California is one of the most significant and important social experiments of the twentieth century. No one who is interested in the intellectual and spiritual future of humanity can fail to take a lively interest in your achievements.

Professor Lord Robbins, 1965

*Visiting Berkeley some twelve years ago, I strolled of a Sunday
afternoon over the campus here .... over Strawberry Creek, then past
the Campanile, down by the library and back out Sather Gate .... That
Sunday I was overwhelmed by the thought that I loved this place,
this campus — the paths, trees, flowers, buildings....*

John Kenneth Galbraith

The Esplanade

Campanile chimes

I am one who has watched the University's rise to the front ranks of world universities with pride and admiration. You have combined here a passion for excellence, the strong support of your governor and legislators and the affection of the people of this state to build a university system which adds luster to California.

Secretary of State Dean Rusk, 1961

Morrison Reading Room, Doe Library

Students of every race will be attracted to this university. The Occident and the Orient, the past and the present will here commingle their culture, and the Pacific will be illumined from Berkeley.

Arthur Rodgers, Commencement address, 1883

Durham Studio Theater

*Berkeley — the University — seems to me more and more to
be California's highest, most articulate idea of itself, the most
coherent — perhaps the only coherent — expression of the
California possibility.*

Joan Didion

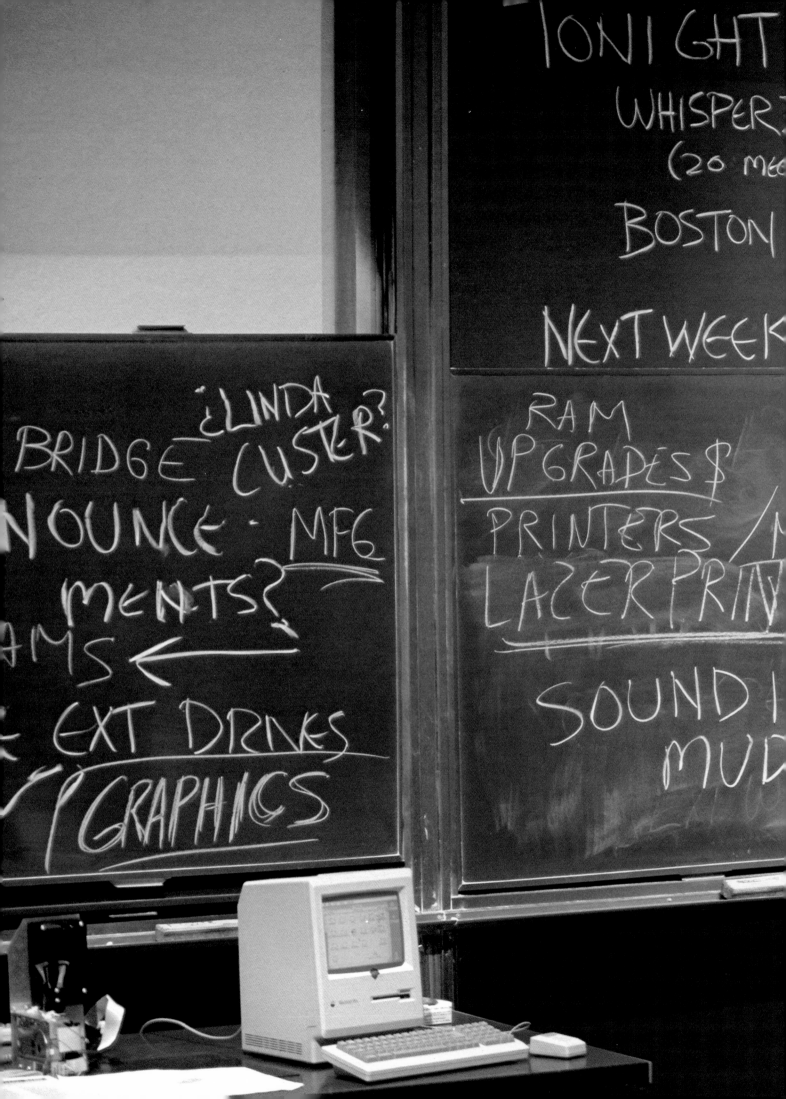

PICK UP A
RAFFLE TICKET!

MAC PLUS - 12...
IMAGEWRITER IIs - 440.°°
    with CABLE
800 K EXT. DRIVE'S - 195.°°
                    - 725.00
HD 20's
BMUG COLLECTIVE BUYING Prices

NEW

NAL SCSI)

UNG

ATIVE):   BORLAND MAC
          TURBO PASCAL

CALL TERR
486-014

MACPASCAL
BOOKS
Best BUY

BAND
MS$

HARD
DISKS

WE C
HE
A

WRITE NOW

E-SCREEN

ERY MAC $?
     BACKUP $
   NOW SYSTEMS

LASER SPOOL

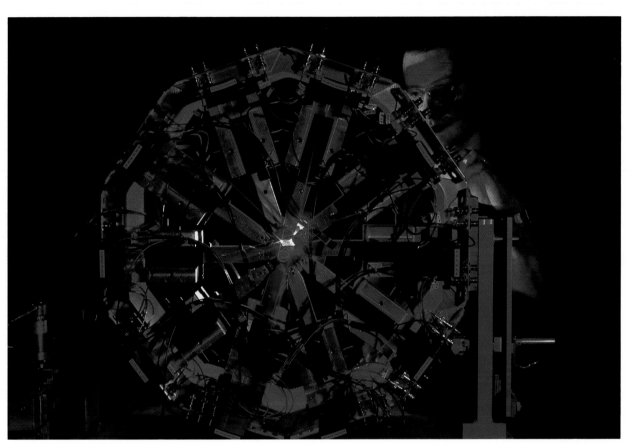

Lawrence Berkeley Laboratory

This University throughout its history has been the single state university most free from external political control and has also become, by any calculation, the leading state university in the nation.

Clark Kerr, 1959

Doe Library

San Francisco Bay

Cal competes in all major men's and women's NCAA Division 1 sports, as well as many club sports.

California has decided that the University shall be the highest type of excellence in everything pertaining to education.

Henry Douglas Bacon

Harmon Gymnasium

I am as proud of my university today as I have always been since I carried logs and boxes to the bonfire in this Greek Theater for the Freshman Rally so many years ago .... The people of California love their University. They rely on it. They trust it .... We citizens of California, fathers, mothers, alumni, must have a vision for our University and a determination that it shall always be second to none.

Chief Justice Earl Warren, 1954

Hearst Greek Theatre / Stanford Candlelight Rally

75

At a luncheon I attended here on campus this noontime, one of your professors asked me where I had gone to college.
I replied, "Harvard."
And he said, "Oh yes, the Berkeley of the East."
Well I could only reply that when I was young I actually considered applying to this university for admission. But I finally decided I didn't want to go to a big-time football school, so I chose Harvard instead.

Sen. Edward M. Kennedy, 1975

The Stanford Axe

Rush Week

By nine o'clock we were in Berkeley...one or two steps inside and we were in fairyland...greenswards in front of classical structures, a running brook, magnificent shrubs and ferns, winding paths under tall, fragrant eucalyptus trees that led up a slight incline to a series of white stone buildings glistening in the sunlight against poppy-covered hills....

Then my mother turned to me.

"Son," she said, "you have to give me your word of honor. I may not be here to see it, and I may not be able to help you, but today you must promise me that no matter what happens to you, you will come to this college."

There was a burning intensity in her voice. Though I was too young to understand the hunger and ambition behind it, I was deeply moved.

" I promise, Ma."

Irving Stone, in *Let There Be Light*, 1970

THE UNIVERSITY OF CALIFORNIA
PHOTOGRAPHS FROM THE PAST

An 1888 view of the Berkeley campus, looking northwest
from the corner of Dana Street and Allston Way.

Looking east in 1874, one sees North and South Halls on the Berkeley campus.

President Wheeler addresses students for the first time at the flagpole, October 3, 1899.

Monday, April 17, 1899 — The Stanford Axe is paraded around the campus for the first time, held by "Lol" Pringle.

President Gilman addresses students in North Hall, April, 1874.

The 36" telescope at the Lick Observatory, Mt. Hamilton, 1890.

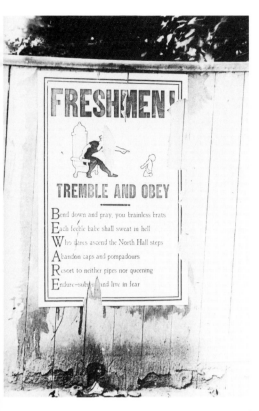

Sophomore warning to freshmen, 1916.

Football rooting section, 1899.

Hazing at the Delta Upsilon fraternity, ca. 1900.

Battalion crossing Shattuck Avenue at Center Street, 1912.

"The Joint" in North Hall, 1913.

In 1914 the granite shell of the Campanile was half-complete.

The 1920 Cal football team before the Big Game, won by Cal 38 - 0.

The stadium filled to capacity for the Big Game, 1924.

Women's P.E. class, ca. 1920.

The 1928 Cal crew receiving the victory wreath in the Olympic Games at Amsterdam.

Skull and Keys initiation on Telegraph Avenue, 1921.

Sather Gate and the campus in 1928.

The President's House, 1933.

The 1937 Freshman - Sophomore Brawl on the field west of Hilgard Hall.

J. Robert Oppenheimer and UC are given awards for the Manhattan Project in 1945.
With Oppenheimer (left) are Gen. Leslie Groves and President Sproul.

The 1948 Cal crew at Henley, August 1948.

Coach Ray Willsey gets a ride after Cal captures the Axe in 1967.

With vision clear we should stand guard and point the way for business of higher standards, for even-handed justice, for unstinted service, for the life more abundant. In that great work it is the University's opportunity to guide, to direct, and to lead.

Robert Gordon Sproul

President Emeritus and Mrs. Robert Sproul place a time capsule into the ground, March 23, 1968.

Berkeley Nobel Laureates in 1960 (left to right): Owen Chamberlain, Edwin M. McMillan, William F. Giauque, John H. Northrup, Wendell M. Stanley, Emilio G. Segre and Glenn T. Seaborg.

President Kennedy leaving the stadium after his Charter Day speech, 1962.

To be public, to be big and to be the best in scholarly competition with the great private universities is a rare achievement. It reflects a subtle passion among faculty, staff, students, alumni, and friends of this place to prove public higher education can also be the best.

Ira Michael Heyman